The Astronaut's Wife:
Poems of Eros and Thanatos
by Lorette C. Luzajic

cover art: Night Light by Iaian Greenson
iaiangreenson@gmail.com
cover design and layout: Raquel Grand
www.raquelgrand.com
photos: Gonzalo Cardenas

Handymaiden Press

www.thegirlcanwrite.Net

ISBN 978-1-84728-733-5

for the men who have made me who I am:
the preacher's daughter, the shaman's sister, the astronaut's wife

for Dad, my greatly cherished Robert Thiessen, my first foundation

and for Robert John Ashley Calvin Thiessen,
my twin who is not my twin,

and for my beloved Marko Nikola Luzajic
1974-2005: my soul mate, husband, friend.
Sail in peace, my astronaut and sailor, I love you and I'm right beside you.
You were most at home on the sea because it is made of my tears.

We don't usually place eternity in our list of needs,
but the soul is only half satisfied with the things of this world.
–Thomas Moore

table of contents

part 1: love

part 2: death

Part 1: LOVE

Yea, though I walk through the valley of the shadow of death,
I shall fear no evil, for thou art with me.
Psalm 23:4

my little brother shows me easter

there on the deck in the fading day of brittle spring
you let me see the moon
you held the telescope just so   and   then   just so
and I might have given up looking for her –
I kept getting my eyes tangled in
trees, on the crackling grey paint on the side of a barn door.
I was shivering from cold

also from the spell of this great orange, rising, rising,
turning the billion-mile sky teal and finally,
shimmering hematite.
At the bottom of the sky,
the moon is almost red and then, at the top she is a transparent frost,
the clearest, cleanest silver.   I cannot look away.

You are fixing and turning and adjusting
doing science and mechanical stuff with the tripod,
working in the few minutes left to catch this particular moon,

this moon only comes once a year, you say,
squinting into the telescope's gaze. It amazes me
how easily you unravel science, learn naturally the tools
with which to pry inside her.
You are gentle with her secrets,
asking simply, humbly to be led inside.
This reverence for God's creation astounds me.
Tonight, you are doing this for me,
to show me what I will never see in the city,
                where you say I am walled.

I put my eye again up to the telescope,
expecting quivery branches in a blurry sky.
Instead   I see a serene fire
(the hollow mystery of craters)
– tears sprang forth at this unexpected intimacy,

at how close   I felt   to something actually out of this world.

(Earlier we were talking. We walked and walked and walked past fruit trees waiting on spring. We walked down to the creek and I wondered out loud to you how I could continue to live without listening to running water. It was a grayish creek with few special features, but sometimes all you really need is water and a few trees. I point out how some plastic bags had blown here, how they are now stuck eerily like hanged men to branches of a naked tree. You look out through the orchards behind the creek, on top of the wind in the plastic like flags. You look right through them and right through everything and tell me they are just corporate ghosts, blowing in the wind.)

Skin

I am caught on the skin
you showed me, upstairs
where I first touched you
curious
and unimaginably lonely.

Star

There in Alabama
with you stretched out in the stars
on someone else's land,
I loved everything.

My pockets were empty,
but I was someone else entirely then.

Prison Blues

more and more now,
in the pain of the morning snow
I miss the flicker of your salamander tongue
and at night, hard green apples
a shared ritual, how we compared juice, firmness
crunch.
and yes it's easy, on a Sunday
to miss you.
– the lonely chill of frosty daylight
feels sentimental, and does not recall
how we wrung each other into total emptiness.

November does not ask questions
about tears and betrayals and lies,
it only mourns your absence and begs the silk
of your belly for her lazy cheek.
more and more, as winter leaks through the window panes
I reach for you in the empty space of my sleep,
wondering if anyone will ever reach for me
the way you reach for me
forgetting, for blessed seconds, the danger of you,
the way your hands pulled strings and
orchestrated my steps, how seductively
they fastened a scarf over my eyes.

and yes of course I know
in forgetting and remembering
that no one's intention is to hurt another –

love simply longs to possess another,
to keep them with a jailer's hands.

Distraction

Lying here between my lover
and the spectre
of his wife
I can think only of
Greek salad
of grilled shrimp
in buttery garlic.

Claire

she's so sad in red
pressing that tiny diamond
into your worn leather palm.

The Book of Salt

After one year pressed so closely against the warm skin of you,
I question everything.
All the words and whispers
    we floated on,   as if there is

security or strength in clouds,
as if love's blinding vocabulary of poems
could mean anything to the lost.

All the injuries we healed together
re-open silently   under a sky of lonely stars.

I wanted to read you, and never put you down.
We spread ourselves like a picnic
before one another,
the strange, unsettled flavours of the other
delicious and sad.

How do I abandon the salt and bread of you,
which has kept me alive?

I have turned myself upside down
to give you love I didn't know I had,
to rest your stunned heart against the open ocean of my soul.
But I always said,   love isn't enough:
you longed to prove it could be.

How eerie the discovery of sorrow
in the light that promised cover from the night.

I cannot read you now,
the ending changes with every page I turn –
every poem of yours I open
challenges the things I thought were certain.

If only I had believed, as you did, that we could overcome
the darkness of the things that made us
before we were each other's.

Daily Bread

It isn't that she's gone blind,
It's only that scarlet things
don't exist, in her mind,
Anyway, they aren't forever,
she insists,
and draws, and turns out lists.

In the surplus of the weather
Sifting through your wholesome grains
I feel like it is Sunday
And I feed on bread and rain.

Poem for Vince (a spell against sadness)
for Donnarama

oh God how I wanted
to be a poet and a rock star a stripper
and a shrink an artist
a missionary   how I wanted
to have something
that the rest of the world
might notice
how I never wanted to care
what anybody thought
of anything

oh baby doll, it's all about
staying alive

falling apart on your floor last night
with fat April and
Sylvester
turning their
yellow-eyed disdain on us
consenting to a brief purr
us being out of
our minds as usual
I wake up wrapped in my dirty old red coat
all the glamour of last night's liquor and perfume
is a sticky film on our skins

and I go

oh baby doll I hope you get out of here
I want you to see the sights
I want everything to blow your mind
I want crowds for you
applause
I want everything that you ever needed
to be real

I'll meet up with you
in New Orleans
for whiskey sours
in a dim jazz bar
where absinthe once drenched the floors
where whores and voodoo queens made
their trades
no one will recognize us in our Gucci shades –
we will get into trouble
raise a few eyebrows and a little hell
don't you worry baby doll,
I am there
when you least expect it in this fucking world
I will be there
you will look up from your cab on Broadway
and see someone wrapped in pink velveteen
crossing the street and you will smile
you will recall stealing ghetto rags from the Goodwill
you will hear someone's shrill laugh in a club and
you will laugh and that is
where I am
right there

remember:
once how trashed after the club
all the queens soaked in root beer shooters
drenched in late night madness and beats
you and me ran back to my house
with our little horde of marijuana
I was standing like a preacher
waving my arms
yelling about how Courtney Love fell into
the warm blood of the man she loved
feeling how dead he was how we bawled there
leaking stark and sour tears over laughter
our sad strength for Kurt Cobain who didn't make it

The Astronaut's Wife

oh baby doll it's all about
staying alive
honey honey honey
let me hear you on guitar
I hear you play alone at night
training your fingers to go where the sound comes from
I hear your crowd go wild when you come on stage
dressed in drag your own designs
Salvation Armani
dressed up as your heroes
Barbra Barbie Garbage
I watch the spell you weave and know for sure
know for certain
how you of anyone I love
how you can do absolutely anything you damn well please
how you can do anything you want to
in this fucking world
shine on, you crazy diamond.

Yemaya Will Make Me a Mermaid

Yemaya will make me a mermaid
when I finally lose touch with this earth
so please spill my soul into open ocean
scatter my ashes on foam
she will gather my ashes with fishes
and spin from them seaweed and sponge
she'll weave my hair in seashells and beads
and kiss me with currents as warm as the sun.

Damage

You pace along the drizzling streets of October,
and your thoughts are winding storms.

You can't be sure he is prepared for the life of a poet,
for the rain-soaked rooms your soul hides.

It has never been other men that your lovers have envied,
but intangible threats like orphans and the sea.

How now, love? after sealing yourself
from its seething gutters and radiant suns,
after shutting down the heart, even the body?
Live by experience
is already your epitaph.

You can't be certain, but you believe he sees how you see.
Still, you fear those less complicated,
shiny girls with firm handfuls of thigh, smooth and poreless,
breasts that rise effortlessly, unbound.

You recall too closely
how fleeting the seduction of your madness,
how damaging your damage,
how you are addictive, then   purged,

how they resent the crash   after the delirium of you,

how quickly men tire of humans.

For Rory, Moving to India to Follow His Buddhist Path

Now that you are leaving,
I am losing you to lepers and Lamas and
rituals I can't understand,
and I'm trying not to see it as just another loss, or another test,
though I could argue effectively
that I need you more than the impoverished millions you will pray for.
You will bypass the further sketches of gossiping queens, overdoses,
and broken hearts,
but you must know how your presence here
kept everybody sane.

After my lifelong friend John died at 31 this spring, his sister wrote
saying she could now understand the purpose of monks and contemplatives,
because while she and I had to keep going, had to work or look after children,
fix supper for the living after weaving through traffic,
while all of this kept on as if nothing had happened,
someone had to mourn the sadness of the world
to let the rest of us go on.

You are that person, called to some greater peace
than I can feel or give. From late night raves to the monastery
is hardly a stretch to those who knew you well:
you were always looking after everyone else
and now,   you must look after the world.

I will miss you on Fridays and on Sunday afternoons,
and on Tuesdays, too,
when my little mood pills aren't working and no one wants to listen
I will miss you when someone turns the music up
and when someone else breaks my heart by dying
or when I don't know what to say or do,
and you would know.

On this side of the world,
there will be a giant hole
but here, in the quiet raging ocean of my messed up heart,
there will be a place of calm that you created there.

Don't look back, soft friend, look forward
Do not look back for sun or rain or war
Follow the moon to the Tibetan night
You were meant for something more.

Valium for Breakfast

for Iaian Greenson

Since you asked, Iaian, I'll tell you
what has become of me, and none of it will
come as a surprise. Tonight on a Friday
I will write this for you.

I can't deal with sordid clubs
or cat barf and dirty socks. And I can't seem
to get into the "new series" –
isn't there an endless stream of new series?

My thoughts are scattered tonight: I am
wondering why my orange kitten
always has such dirty little feet. I think,
well, I'm fat and I work as a cashier,
just as Satan promised me on Highway 61.
I think, money, how there isn't any,
unimaginably less than zero.
And I think, my friend,
that love is a sick delusion: I read
graffiti that said so on a bathroom wall.
Love, its quiet scars, its gaping maw, how
I fell in and drowned and now I'm just a ghost,
writing to you, telling you
what has become of me,
because you asked.

And it's Valium for breakfast
and vitamins for lunch
and yoga on Sundays and
therapy on Wednesday afternoons.
And I might not come out often
but you know just where to find me
you could write out my heart like a poem.

Hands

Hands,   hundreds

hunting

   holding

he helped her hunger
helpless, hapless, hopeless
hunger

     (he
      happened
      heaven)

Home for the Holidays

I don't want to be at home for Christmas
I want to be away
and experience snow and singing
in my own cathedral, on a different street
apart from the familiar voices in our house.
Take the smiles from your faces,
I read through them long ago,
and now I'm tired and ready to fall apart.

I don't want to be at home for Christmas
– do you suppose I feel safe here?
I love you but am afraid that will never be enough
and I can't take it anymore,
I can't take it anymore.

Mother wrap me up
Don't you see I'm cold?
Father, don't push me down
I'm seventeen and old.

Caramel

Your skin is
lush and caramel
spreading itself across me
like fondue.

Darwin's Mistake

The soft sums of our years have jagged edges
a jigsaw for ragged hopefuls
and those not yet poisoned by a drug like hope.
Who can, after all, unravel fate's dole
and especially, fate's debt?

I feel the sure sad footing beneath me, of acceptance,
a glimpse of future strength, smile in recollection: a song:
James: *I don't believe that love must mean despair*
how we wanted to believe such a thing, how we did try everything
want everything and fail miserably, give everything and fall,
fall apart, fallen
(I put in everything I had, my love, and my hands are empty.)
We ripped each other to shreds.

One day I will accept all of this as a story the cosmos spun for fun,
a sacred time of intensity meant
to make us know the things we need to know,
a chance to thrill at life and meet her jesters.
I will feel what an honour it was to be loved,
to be loved so wildly with nothing restrained,
to open the dark torrents of myself to you,
fill up my mind with another's without reserve.
Who wouldn't give anything at all,
everything they own and have and know –
for a single day like that?

Clearly,
the hurt heart is all of literature,
it is nothing new or unique to our story
that skin and bones
are made of sorrow.

I would never look back at all
were it not for drops of Jupiter and
missing you too much to go further.
How crushing a truth I dare not utter:
that perhaps   love itself
is simply a mistake of evolution.

May

There are still burn marks on my back
from making love to you
on the kitchen floor.
I inhaled dust and onion peels
and sat in kernels of cat food
just to have you faster.

Memory from Louisiana

Did you dream that this would happen?
Did you know my mind would melt into your mouth
when suddenly, out of nowhere, you were pulling
my responses, promises?
I remember the dark bar, the Cajun music,
in that drowning hour.

Did I dream of this
before I touched your skin as young as old
as full of history, mystery,
as the Mississippi river bank
where I undressed you slowly…
I could hardly believe how you felt in my hands…

Who knows where I will run into your hungry eyes again,
when I will have the chance to trace your scars
Forgive me: I could not stay on the street:
I was a tourist, you could say,
from another planet altogether.
You have no idea how I drove to California
searching for you in the pockets of the coast
describing you to punkers who might know you.
That was as far as I could go, the ocean,
and you were not there.
I was about to fall right off the cliffs of the continent
and so,
and only so,
I let you go.

Codependency

What gorgeous, restless crisis
are you bringing to me now?
My hands are full of stars
you've caught and crushed
and my eyes are full of blood
and my mouth is full of soap
and wine
and nails

You dazzle and confound me
your foolishness astounds me
you laugh, and I think of New Orleans
in your tears
I recall blackbirds
and the curious taste
of rust and
            sapphires.

It is Only Now

It is only now
that I can shed in words, your smile
those eyes
that drove me
to the half insanity of want
my eyes
which never told this truth

My arms
were not enough to hold you
and this is why I left you
and that is why
I write this here
where you will never picture
my hands
still occupied
with these old photographs

Missing I. who was Swallowed by the World

First cigarette of the day
and it's 5:55 –
almost held out until tomorrow, or Holland,
where you have gone, disappearing onto a map I have not written.
I am deaf and blind from here
I cannot hear you laugh, or quite picture
the things you might be doing.
I do not wish you were here.
I do not wish you were here.

I went to California, without you.
I did not think of you
when I laid in the arms of strangers
or found God.
I thought of you
when the waves crashed like broken glass shards
against the rocks.
I thought of you when driving past tiny museums,
or drinking whisky in pubs that smelled of your home:
beer and grilled cheese.

There is no definition for us. I dream of you
and long for your presence
in ways not knowable to others
or even to us.
We are friends who feel safe enough
to argue over
the meaning of life.
On both occasions that we held each other,
it was as far as we could go.
We did not want there to be
more to run from.

I wear Bowie out on my stereo tonight
and smoke each cigarette down past the filter.
I feel quiet and generous and sad.
I feel lost because I do not know where you are.
You promised you would find me,
if you ever return.

Madman on Queen's Park Avenue

I found you eating pomegranates
In the corner of a dusty, crowded room
And I wondered if you'd ever been to Mars
And you turned your hands toward me
They were heavy with gloom
And they seemed to span a million different wars.

I caught you on a busy avenue
With glitter in your eyes
And words spilled from your mouth like noisy quarries
I should have stopped you then and there
And queried your disguise
Never miss a chance to hear another's stories.

Grief

Who were you thinking of
when we made love for the last time,
and do you think of me
when you're with her?

You could never be happy
where you were,
always wanting to be somewhere else,
always wanting to be somebody else.

I rack my brains for reasons
why you stopped seeing my soul
and I come up with a blank black board –
forever couldn't keep me in the restless prison that was you.
It was too good to be true, anyhow,
– love is full of sick and sorry tricks and lies.

Whose delusion was I under
when I believed in our possibilities?
Like sand they have spilled from my hands,
like stars, they are not even there.

Ode to Blue Sky or Sunflower or
Whatever Her Name was in the Florida Café

She smiles of some other sun
the blinding goldenrod of Maryland highways
all those rainbow people, dancing

She sings of some other song
notes of noonday light
touching bird sound
soft and centred

She moves in another May
among marigolds
unburdened burgeoning blossom

she blooms
where barns tumble
and sprout roses.

June Fever

Perhaps he never caught on to
spring's slow ascent into summer
to the heat layering itself between the days and how
it could flatten
your resistances like paper

She

She,

      her,

sweet sweat

      in the red camisole

gently cupping

what my lips

      long

      to sip

Poem for A.

I envision for you sanctuary,
and clean water.
My anger was razor sharp,
but that has been covered in flowers.
I resented you for telling me
I was not who I was
– you who had never looked at me
you who had never cut your hands open
on coloured glass
or stained your skin with strawberries

I wish you abundance
and fresh fruits
damp earthy leaves and glass marble moons
I wish you soft hands and winding stairways
milk-teary icons
magic flutes
warm mouths
I wish you Eden.

Poem for B.

Oh, I've been sad for years, my friend –
it's a painter's fate to feel,
and a writer's lot to live a little lost.
Oh, I've been shedding tears, my friend
'cause this world's way too real,
but the ticket price is truly worth its cost.

I don't have any answers
but I know the answer's light –
truth and joy have meaning,
and life's a worthy fight.

I watch you struggle, darling
I feel the bruise and fight
and I looked straight into darkness
to see a starry night.

And I don't know what to do,
I don't know where to go,
but a warrior went before us
and he says, don't let go.

I could not help falling
and I cannot be wise –
it was likely angels calling
and the rain inside your eyes.

Warning

I'm coming from somewhere that you never were
A platform of integrity and no disguise
Nothing to hide, and nothing, now, to ask
Pity I couldn't see the vampire in your eyes.

The Astronaut's Wife

Every Day is Like Sunday

Don't know when I looked up
and noticed you noticing me
and my heart skipped a beat like a girl still in school
I sure thought you were sweet

and life is chaos and disorder
that I can't seem to get in order
and I see you're bringing the exact same story to me
I'm so busy dodging the holes in the road
my head is down and my heart is closed
still ripped to shreds by losses I can't keep track of anymore

I've liked the winter nights in the little house
how I felt safe inside, beside you
Sundays busting a gut over Simpson foibles
Scrabble mid-week – the only game I play to win
making tea and collages, just to have good company
don't you think it's nice just being who you are?

So, what becomes of questions that didn't need answers,
what to do about the strangeness that making love makes out of friends?
I say just look both ways and open your heart
and come as you are

Well, I'm not going to run and hide
I've broken bread with you
made art and love with you
and still I barely know you at all
you can't keep anyone but you can keep what you become

and if every day is like Sunday
can I spend all my Sundays with you?

The Bus Poem

I been on buses
greyhounds, voyagers, weaving through Rockies
toppling too close to the edge
long and lumbering
rumbling through
the bumbling quiet of Tennessee

I been hungry horny happy
and scared, on buses
I been lonely and loved and lovely
and loathed, on buses

I been shy next to fat Texan women
and their big red nails,
on buses
I been tough and snide
when the cheap California
trash start makin' eyes,
on buses

I been lost out where the blues was born,
on buses
I been blue through swamps
where dark was sliced open by headlights
of buses

I seen the most beautiful black man alive
felt him touch me under an afghan
under my skin
going through Virginia
we did things that ain't legal in Virginia,
on buses

I seen a big lardy chain smokin' nutbar
tried to kill his wife, he said,
thought she was a gook there for a minute
driver ain't said nothing about his smokin'
and drive on, on buses

The Astronaut's Wife

I been on many buses
too many buses
west east north and south buses
october ontario   buses
marshy mississippi   buses
down dizzy canyon   buses
jazzy cajun country   buses

i've been mad sad hunted and haunted
on buses
i've been hard jarred blunted and daunted
on buses

I been on buses.

Summer

Like black
summer rain
she takes the warm new dreamer
born sea blue morning,
we imagined
something more.

Treasures

I found an old piano
in a field of marigolds and corn
It was still haunted
by the hands that it had worn.

New Orleans Jazz Bar

Sunshine shoeshine youshine moonbeam
polished snapper
jazz tapper
you dapper, cane and coat tails
cat tails windsails

you lemon lime thing
super sweet party treat
sax blows
horn flows
trumpet crows
croons tunes of you-me
slap-slapping sweetly into sea

Untitled for A.

You said I was not a poet
yet you never held new kittens in your palm,
or let the blues soak through your skin in Tennessee

I've been many things
the ghost
the artist
the photograph
the lover

You said I was not a starlet
yet you never walked through acid light
and astral planes or swam in crystal waters
for the camera of my eyes

I was never
all those pieces you could not pick off the ground.

Waiting for Malachi

I like lying in the park, lazy, sedated
a smile on my face under my shades

and still
sort of

       waiting

things   slow   down

after weeks of mental frantics my brain frying up all kinds of confusion
and I put those tangles to rest escaped them temporarily but your heartbeat is
somewhere else...
that turns my pulse
all the images memories
flashes heat and tears I ride this wave out to sea find sadness
distress confusioncloaking choking me

I was being pragmatic
when I tried so damn hard
not to fall flat on my face for you
all those toos and buts getting stamped out
smoldered by you   sweat
and then

by your stories

I learn each day as I try to transcend my frustrations and what-ifs. I keep them
in check cause chances are I'll never find you declare your arms again in this
wilderness of people and no real leads

I'm scared of that, but not as scared as I am of

falling

       flat on my face for you

slam hard
can't seem to get up
no, not even 2000 miles from where I left you
I know you're out there

The Astronaut's Wife

Minnesota Marlboro Montana
L.A. Louisiana, lakes, lowlands
lovers telepathics telling little lies
you think of me you wait for me they say
but where?

I have looked for you in all these places
but beads and palms and
poets, vampires
dark slouched lost people
vendors canyons bars reservations later,
I know I search for me as well.

This story is a play I play with words
to avoid running from
while running to

change has been my way of life
but it still scares a coward with neuroses left to lose

I take my words with me
and perhaps someday you'll read them
in a quiet café
a newspaper or zine
left behind on someone's soiled tray
and I hope it won't be long
because then you'll understand
because then you'll understand

and I know that you are lonely
because I am.

The High Priestess

This is a poem for the girl
who dreamed of trains
and a man falling in the garden,
a girl whose broken hourglass
signaled new life instead of doom.
Some phoenixes rise instead of just pretending,
though it is hard to find maps that show
the way out of ourselves…
better to find the way inward via moon light,
through dark synapses and long cave corridors
that silently lead to the heart of Christ.
The enemy is hard to exorcise,
but the high priestess finds her wisdom
by listening to the games of her very own mind.

I will miss this girl
who has shown me that the way to freedom
is an open heart and a strong mind.
This is the girl who stood in her own shadow and
commanded it
to her word.
Through nightmares of attic laboratories
and cockroaches that flowed like bloody highways
under her skin,
she will rise.
She will find her place in the mountains
and the fresh air and Eden's sea
will nourish her fragile bones.
Her eyes will fill with the planets,
new and ancient,
it is her
amber shell
that preserves the secrets of light.

We are Not Birds

1.

On Sunday mornings, after making love,
she examines her flesh, the soft expanse of thigh
and imagines sinew, circulation, genetic disorder.
Inside the familiar skin she has come to recognize as "me"
are a million systems, arteries and maps,
blueprints   for neurochemical disasters.
She is half Mother's, the peasant hips,
the extra nourishment for unignited eggs-
and half his –   inside this wavering temple,
this archeology of salt –
half his   a straight line.

And where should she start, undoing the damages?
Where does she begin
to point accusations?
Perhaps it is always better
to let time's gravity erase
what never should have been history.

After all, whatever,
everyone is damaged, everyone's
in some kind of therapy,
some kind of addict, some kind of neurotic anomaly,
everyone is grappling to put the pieces back together
and it's nothing new –
saints and sorcerers, doctors, lawyers, shrinks and pills
powders and rolled-up bills,
churches and talk shows
priests and Buddhas.

On Haitian hillsides, baskets of apples appease the ancestors,
bowls of mangoes beg the blessings of the Divine.
We've been talking
to the dead for so long
that it's hard to hear the living.

2.

The girl held out an olive branch
and vowed to stop blaming them
for every last thing that went wrong in her world.
At some point, we must make a point of forgetting
submerge harm, expose it to love.

(and some to whom she gave herself
were vampires,

and some were owls
wise souls who could see in the dark.)

3.

And so what if the girl identifies with refugees and orphans,
if she sees shadows in the corridors of her bright imagination?
So what if she is a peculiar little girl
in caves of books and a halfway house for the broken?
Once, after Christmas dinner, her husband asked:
What have they done to you? What the fuck did they do to you, baby?

4.

She looks for her selves on maps,
unscrolling the intestinal mass of brain and winding it carefully
on labeled spools   she understands serotonin and synapses,
has unravelled the mystery of the hypothalamus, the amygdala.
Dendrites are her favourite; she watches the whole of her childhood
course through their outstretched fingers,
 processing, plugging.

Anxiety has ceased to be a feeling- she has compartmentalized it
to science. My dopamine levels are low today.
Tryptophan, norepinephrene.

She is sure she can find her mother here, too,
where she has spent decades looking,
following the charts that describe schizophrenia, mania, borderline personality,
narcissism, bipolar madness.
There is comfort in unravelling it this way;
the clinical and medical are cleaner than
the unpredictable past,
the yelling and screaming, the way that little girl shrunk
beneath the blustery nerves,
how she hid under blankets, and blankets of poems
in that dark house.

5.

(I can forgive all this, with my medical books
and pill bibles,
I can decipher you if I can decipher me.
Still, the eeriest agony is observing
 the forgotten one,

the one who endured for me, for us, for his other children,
the neglect and disarray.

The story you tell is different,
but my memory yields up nothing but his love.

Day in and day out, I watched the long blue wagon
backing out of the long driveway,
    watched him drive off to the noisy factory.

The house was so crowded with clutter,
with obsessive mounds of Christmas baubles,
junk mail, endless paper tubes and
magazines, rooms without people,
rooms brimming with junk,
cardboard boxes, rancid cosmetics, endless piles of fabric,
endless piles, heaps, endless,
endless, swallowing every surface, endless papers, endless
halls of endless junk, sucking up every square inch of space,
endless, swallowing, swallowing.
Nothing that comes into that house can ever leave.

What I can't forgive is this:
that there is so much stuff,
there is no room left for my father.)

6.

How strong he was
How noble and dutiful a captain
at the helm of their sinking Titanic.

7.

and A, how his handsome youth
is falsely hardened by seven scars
(from the night the chemistry experiment backfired,
broken glass shockingly close to the eye, the jugular
– how much she almost lost.)

A, lost in muddy ponds and the flight of moths,
a speck in his constellations and concentrations,
bug wings and goldfish.
Now, seventeen,
he is a gardener   of marijuana.
This strain has smaller leaves and thicker buds.
It's a smoother blend, with a faint taste of apples.

When he is humiliated under perpetual false blame,
the girl cannot stand the trip back in time, to the times she stood in his shoes.
(selfish selfish selfish selfish selfish)

The two of them discuss themselves while watching Simpsons,
how they have been drawn and what their script is.
The girl has been blamed for indoctrinating him
with drugs and anti-corporatism.
Truth is, he came to think all on his own.
(How closely our DNA must match! We are twins
who are not twins.)

8.

It is perhaps best between the sisters
that they do not speak often
and certainly not at any length, on issues of any importance.
Yet there is no lack of love, simply the wisdom not to argue.
As children, they were cold and calculating. She could not forgive
her sister's reckless resentment, her schemes and manipulations,
her lies, her teenage addiction
to stealing makeup and stickers.
She held a grudge against her for being the favourite,
(God forgive me.)
How long the girl took for granted her sister's strength,
for being the older one,
for holding the family together while Dad worked.
Cooking, cleaning, delegating chores.
Age seven, age ten.

9.

(Sometimes D. envies my wild freedom,
my childlessness and heart without roots.
She can't grasp abstract thought and
longs to understand the poems I've written,
to sense what things I am painting about, what they mean.
She wonders sometimes,
if I'm lucky in my life without boundaries.
She secretly believes that my friends are more interesting.

Don't think I don't see what you have built. Don't think I don't know
that you have made the best investments. The quiet quilt of your life
is the centre of what's left of us.)

D. is the family candidate with the best chance for happiness,
despite the insecurities she sees in the mirror.
Ordinary is stability.
Flight means fall for all human species.
We are not birds.

10.

Perhaps there will always be denial and broken hearts. It is possible
that things will never get better, and it is possible that that does not matter.
Mom will have her garden and her geese, and find contentment
in planting jalepenos and beautiful roses.
And A's ideas of political or personal freedom can't be realized
in this world, but still, he made it this far,
unlike the kid next door who turned seventeen and hung himself
in the basement.
A. will be okay,
his compassion for others will guide him.
And Dad, whose world feels like a crumpled newspaper,
will be judged before God with nothing to hide:
kind, strong, generous, loyal, a man of his word.
D. will take on the Christmas dinner, the housework,
the care and feeding of the young, as she always has.

And the girl, even with her peculiar blend of nervousness,
and losses she cannot count,
has freedom and art.

We are not birds, our backs have never broken into wing
we are suspended below the heavens,
we cannot know the verb to soar.
Gravity holds us in place,
our genes sift randomly:
each DNA cell
a gorgeous chaos that is,   in the end
only ashes after all.

Part 2: DEATH

And Jesus said,
"I tell you the truth, today you will be with me in paradise."
Luke 23:43

Hope

It is your eyes
that give way to light
despite the shield of tears
and salt-stained lashes.
I said to you,
hope might be the most dangerous drug,
and you said, yes,
but not so lethal
as its absence.

Sapphire

gloomy burdens
go out with the trash tonight
you, glittering
and broken among them,
my most pathetic vice.

Incest

the girl I hung out with at age six

     (was it that long ago that we pulled each other

up and

    down
in
    splintering

red

wagons

    and ate sand and raspberries
    from my grandmother's back yard?)

yeah, it's been a long time and

now
I read about her in the paper

    ran off to the city
    found in an alley
    still young and fragile

her guts

    rotted out

    on the pavement.

Jesus Wept

When Jesus wept,
He cried for all the unborn children
and the doom and gloom they were in for
the concave stomachs and the flies
the back of father's hand: the lies

He ate with women
we would not walk with
listened patiently for hours
dried their tears and gave them flowers
relieved them of their scars and thirst for pain
prayed for water, blood and rain

Something had to be done
about a man who called himself God
went around praying with hookers
had an unmarried mother.

Something had to be done
something driven through hands and feet
something stolen from his sleep
nails to keep him where everyone could see
but Jesus only said,
pick up your cross, and follow me.

The Scarecrow (for Matthew Shepard)

With you pinned up in the sky
like a scarecrow in a field of apples,
knowing for hours you were going to die,
it was almost Christian
how you gave up the ghost.
You were a bruised light
tethered and
softer than a pale blue dust shard.
You were psychedelic in the papers,
as they whirled you into hero, target
victim, saviour, shame.
Yet you were only the Hanged Man,
baffled by the things that this world lacks,
how few devices in it left to save you.

November

She is not there to interrupt your mythologies –
nor will she interpret them for you.
She waits for you to spin these multiple causations
out of comfort or need
– she waits patiently, absorbing more than you know.
You shudder. Love is an alien.

Still, you are here
and you do not wish to leave.
You cannot tell what she remembers,
what expressions or fragility or dreams she recalls from your narratives.
But I know, so let me tell you:
she recalls everything,
even the thick red slab
of your beautiful thigh.

Scenario:
dark, abandoned, charred mansion
sounds: rats, perhaps djinn, strange shuffling movements
a woman sobbing
no – it is not grief

Flashback:
a child spills sugar
after shaky hands let slip the jar
a woman shrieks
a child is burned
sealed forever with warnings tattooed onto his brown hand.
Now he is much older,
the scar, the hand,
look lonely
across her skin.

Movie:
man strolls down the urban street
long hair and leather, confident and hard.
He chats up girl outside club.
She leaves her friend inside, without knowing why,
just that she has to,
and goes with passerby.
Winter passes with venom
and frail pride.

Elegy

Sometimes she must change continents
move
try an Italian accent with her latte
or hide behind trees.

She was always somewhere
beating drums in the Amazon
wearing necklaces of tooth and horn
and late for dinner.
They would try to catch her
their nets and searchlights helpless
against the world map,
the thick and spicy incense of Africa
the silver jangling at Mexican roadsides.

After her death,
I saw her once,
hitch-hiking down a slow hot Mississippi highway.
The crimson sky stained the cotton fields bloody
on either side of that dusty ribbon.
I was weaving past scattered porches.
Someone was wailing the blues.

ghosts

ran into rain down on the corner
she was down and out
and a little uneven
I tipped my hat and smiled
for "even the rain has such small hands"

at night I dreamed of mangoes
feared all kinds of seeds

ran into spring tomorrow night
felt her breathing rustling bustle
windy and a little lost
so soft inside my palms

Portrait of Elaine in the Sun

(this poem was written when I was 16 yrs old,
a few months before Elaine Bown was murdered in Toronto)

Black
salvation army black
head shaved partly
red hair up
black eyeliner
punk

Rebelling for her freedom
perhaps the freedom she embraces now
a solitary moment
on the hill
unaware than anyone watches
the sun pouring generously
on her stark and stunning face

In a Place in Fonthill

In a place in Fonthill there are little white crosses
and there rests my friend Elaine Bown
in all of my life I have known many losses
but none of them have I found
to be quite the loss that her death was to me
I loved her, she was different and bold
Some say that Elaine has gone home to be free
I can't believe what I'm told.

Oh, you murderers, so full of hate
what right have you to decide her fate?

Oh, this earth is a rude place, a crude place
where man dares to spite and cause pain
He will not suffer guilt over what he has killed
over the life he has slain.

Elaine, you died in vain
and no one seems to care
they say you suffered pain,
but that it happens everywhere.

But girl, you didn't live alone
your short life had a reason
oh, what anguish I have known
Life is a bitter season.

For Elaine, a Mermaid

There are claws across her face like bands
and miles and miles in her eyes
the stars bite into her frozen hands
she's shining in the moonlit skies.

I called her name, it sounded silver
on my slivered tongue, a gorgeous sound
she shivered in that fiery river
so terrified of being found.

In dreams, she is an orphan
in day dreams, she is by the sea
I begged for her like she were morphine
and dreamed that she came home to me.

Eulogy for Carmine Lowe

May a thousand blooms
grow out of you
so that you return to Eden
without loneliness.

May God be just in judging you
and take into account the time
we sat together on your Great Dane's bed
and looked out through the windows
at His stars.

Flowers from Carmine

Who knows who you are
or why you keep yourself sane
by collecting dogs and lunchboxes

You love to talk on about this and that
and never disclose much
in these ramblings

I've lived half as long as you have
and I haven't lived as hard,
but I don't have a garden.
Your bouquets are startling – colour like spring
erasing used up seasons.

I imagine you at night, trowel in hand,
digging through the pieces of your life
weeding out what is broken or dead.
You meditate in secret
on the colours that you and rain created.

But these are just my imagined pictures. I am one of those types who spends too
much time alone in cafes. It's the caffeine that does it to me. I put too much store
in the unknown, in multiple causation. And you – you could not analyze me if
you tried.

Your invitations to smoke grass are uneasy but eager.
You like me because you do not scare me,
and because there is something left in me
that can still surprise you.

But we will never really know each other. I will lose you.
I would ask for more from you but you do not ask for more friends.

I picked a rose while walking home one summer night,
a treasure
from your quiet yard.
I wore it, like a gift, in my hair.

Bad

bad boys
smoke dope wear sneakers and black leather
nowadays add pants that hang below crotch level
and ugly hats

but bad men
slink around in olive suits and
gold watches
and read beat junk on the subway

bad girls
sit on buses, back seat window
with sunglasses and blackberry lips

bad women
write Bernardo letters in prison
and think
how close to death
they have never been

In Managua

(for J, who was left behind)

On a lazy, sunny afternoon
an American garage.
Bob Seger on a dusty radio.
You fixed our pick-up.
I never connected with men who were rugged,
whose women called them *old man*.
Death by wheels, your leather said.
Big Daddy-o, with three Spanish babies in your arms.
You could outrun your lovers, helicopters, cops,
LSD, moonshine and Texas-
but not your own wheels.

I trust the cliff that swallowed you
had the tough assed strength
of the women you loved.
I trust God will give something
to keep the children you left
in sunlight.
I trust He will give you
new wheels.

With All Due Respect, Mr Thompson (1939-2005)

Thousands will be writing for Hunter
like for Kennedy and Lennon and Di
as if the drunken old sod were a hero
as if he was genius while high.

I wish I were able to tell you
that the things I have seen on my own
would make Wilde look mild
and Hunter look tired
and require a fabulous gown.

The Pomegranate Eater

A pomegranate drips seeds
and the shell yields its flesh to
the spongy crunch of its insides –
somewhere a bitter foam
seeps from your body
like the fruit which you devour.
Your stained face
reveals more than you know.

How could I have known
that I am anchorless,
that I have been a wounded bird,
abandoned by the very salt that heaved me,
exposed and friendless,
onto the shore?

Did you ever think about the world you gave me?
How fish and centipedes and dandelions
would crowd out your creation? How anyone would cower
under your hissing and uncharitable lies?
Only now does it all unravel
only now does this bruised skin
give way to light.

Cult of Diana

Diana
goddess of the hunted
you gaze at us
from the watery lens of the grave

some say
they see you
healing others
lighting up the sky
a ghost before you are cold

huntcircles
will appear in fields
strange lights
planets will be named for you
no one will remember why,
or how it happened that way

whatfor is the blue dot
of your smiling Bradbury eyes

Next Door

Next door to where I lived out all my childhood
mysteries in creeks and forts and the books
beneath my bed,
Kurt Cobain took another casualty.
A young boy nailed himself into his room
strung a rope
and jumped.

My brother was eight at that time
it was his first experience of death
not the passing a grandparent whose health became frail
but this,
this mother screaming for days for release
this boy
whose raven hair was long and silk
whose eyes were wide and open and
frozen in seventeen.

Everything Tastes Like Crack

everything tastes like crack
now I can't wash the flavour
out of my cigarettes or coffee mugs
the telephone
I've never been a puritan
I have my drugs of choice
everyone does:
TV kills the Net kills smoking kills sex kills
booze kills Prozac kills coffee kills and
crack kills
so what can I tell you?
you who never calls
except now when you heard about
the rock I found behind my house
do I want to come over and play with you?
I guess you didn't hear how I flushed it away
what can I tell you
except to say
I watched at least one family
go down
on crack
I watched cops and robbers
up close and personal
I saw my lover's mama
buy crack from her six foot three son
I watched her fourteen-year-old daughter
carry two babies on her hips
their daddy was another dealer,
her foster daddy.
I watched them with my own eyes
waiting for rock
I watched the scars on Malachi's hands
when he touched me
on a cockroach covered couch
how his tongue tasted bitter of crack
though he had never tasted it
how his skin tasted like
all the sadness of rock-bottom despair
everything everything everything
tastes like crack.

In Memory of Dimitri Kousis

Why and wherefore, what and how
Does always discontent prevail?
Some tawdry tatters haunt the now
The scream, the sleep, how sweet the veil.
Create a summer, watch it fall
Delicious, messy, spun from dew
I'm freezing in this wintry hall
A severed hand apart from you.

Notes on Leaving a Friend

You are dancing,
shrouded in prisms of blue-blonde light
eyes closed, hands empty
swallowed by smoke.

I handed you heart, hands
made up of broken glass
and bloody angels
filthy fingers that had
touched earth, you.
you made them soft,
peeling back the fibres of the palms,
you breathed laughter
I trusted you
I trusted our Tuesday morning wine
and let loneliness dissolve
melting darkness into dawn.

Now, missing you
watching you dance like spun cotton candy
no angles no edges
I am off to the ends of the earth
to Africa
alone with this dazzling picture.

You Never Talked About Dying
(for Dimos)

You never made it back to Greece,
and now there is nothing to keep you
from the white stone shores.

You can float
in sun-drenched eternity
a turquoise ripple in the depths of blue.
In little white houses, there are
        plates of olives and lamb, steaming in wait of you.

You never talked about dying,
but then, what is there to say?
I'm afraid, I'm angry, I'm lost
these are the things
that lay in your heart,   dark shrouds

Of these sorrows inside me, I could not speak,
but you knew,
you knew I was petrified to lose you,
you knew my optimism was for you,
you knew
you could not keep me
from crumpling and

I knew
there was   nothing
I could do
to save you.

Another Poem for Julie Ann

It's a beautiful spring day and Anita is dying.
The first spill of sunshine after a long winter
makes cats stretch and yawn dizzy smiles,
turning their bellies to the window.

One twin will be left with an empty space
beside her where Anita was, once,
all through the womb, the first year of the crib.
Julie Ann doesn't ask why an infant girl has to suffer brain cancer
or why one and not the other. She doesn't expect any miracles
and prepares her heart
as best she can
for goodbye.
She says Anita has already changed the world,
a little girl who doesn't want to stay.

Julie Ann has shared my secrets
for fourteen years, and I hers. She wanted to be a revolutionary.
I wanted to be famous. In quieter ways, perhaps those dreams
did not die. Once at Dead Horse Point,
I was terrified she would fall into the canyon
and I would have to live without her. We couldn't have imagined
a future this way. The ones who came into our lives like
little stars blanketing the dark with pinpoints of heaven, the ones
who fell in, the shrines
we built inside of us to honour them.

I couldn't picture either of us one day as mothers,
Julie Ann with her sack of tools, and my bags of cosmetics and books.
We drove across the United States gnawing on ribs disposed of by hotels,
we collected beads in the sticky streets of New Orleans, picked up hippies
hitching to Phoenix, we searched the world over for love and light and
got lost along the way. How graceless was our transition to adulthood,
in an angry world filled with lies and madness. How I chopped off
half my soul just to avoid all the feelings I couldn't avoid.
We buried friends and lovers and their prison cells and motorcycles.
Julie Ann became such a wise and practical mother.
I never felt apart from her even when I was.

Erica will ask one day about her other half,
the sister whose little body is emptying of life. She will carry
this solemn secret, the identity of being half of twins.
She will resent and treasure being both of them, and carrying her
mother's grief.
I do not have a child, cannot comprehend
the scope of what this means for a mother,
though I have losses of my own,
indeed, it seems life has been nothing but loss.

I can empty myself of words that will never bring Julie Ann
back to the little woman she and Demian created.
I can pray these words to God or fold my Tarot cards and place them
in the earth, and I can offer up my arms
to hold my friend, when hers are half-empty.

Life will go on, the crickets will squeak in the summer night, and
companies will keep pushing their plastic refuse
into the water that babies drink. I have kept count of my losses
in poetry, but it is more important to keep count of today's small gifts,
the restless purr of an orange kitten in a sunbeam,
the kisses of living children, the small scars that carve my
younger brother's handsome face. My nephews will grow, finding their
place under the poisoned skies the way we all do.
Julie Ann will be all right,
but not entirely all right, the way we all are.

Kitty's Garden

1.
I learned from Kitty, 92, that you are always too young to die,
and also, that you can still be ready.

Visiting Kitty was a challenge at first. How her eyes watched me, how they
sponged up every last colour from the flowers. I wheeled her past
yards and talked about their gardens; Kitty knew the names of all the plants
butshe couldn't tell them to me.

This mattered to me, that I could talk and be heard, but Kitty could not.
Still, soon, I found different ways.
I watched her sparky little face for the details.

When it was too cold for escape from the
howling and shouting of the other old people, and from
the smells of gravy and diapers, I brought photos and told Kitty my stories.
My Oma, how funny all the pictures of grandmother are,
her wide owl eyes, her mouth an o. And my brother,
seventeen and insolent. How he likes astronomy: stars and plants, including
marijuana. He wants to be a web master and
master of the skateboard. How he is everything to me.
Here, Kitty, here are my nephews, their baby giggles almost audible.
Kitty's eyes- her arms move out now,
she is reaching for the babies. The boys in the photograph are laughing together
in a laundry basket. One has a blue towel over his head.
My paintings –   Kitty's eyes, Kitty's eyes.   The grey walls in her Leisure World
cell are coloured by Christmas cards and by two paintings.
Already they are shrouded – one I recall distinctly, of a boat.
The other, perhaps geese against a sunset sky.
They are her works, when she could move her hands.
Mine are chaos, like me, rushes of desperate colour and distorted themes.

Kitty disapproves, but is too polite to say so.
She is thinking, she could help me learn to draw,
if only, if only.

More photos – Dimitri. Small and smiling, sunken cheeks, a big grin. I share my
grief with Kitty. This is Dimitri, he died last May, at 25. How I miss him, I miss him.
He died of AIDS: I tell Kitty cancer, not a lie.
Her claws reach for me. She touches my hand. Her eyes are crying.

When the photos are tired, I read from the Bible. Ecclesiastes,
my favourite. It seems suddenly grim,
here in the place where people wait for death.
There is nothing new under the sun.
I halt; and then go on;
there is nothing in death to hide from a 92 year old woman,
who waits for it with the dignity and patience of a saint, without complaint.

One day Kitty tries very hard to speak.
Words are hard, but this is important. I have learned to wait patiently when she
struggles to make words. I have learned to say,
try again, Kitty, I didn't catch it this time. But this time, I understand right away.
Kitty is telling me she loves me.

2.
The inevitable; the phone call. My work there is over.
Kitty's work is over, too, a lady I knew for six months of her 92 years,

my friend.

When the seasons bring the sun, I will go into my mother's garden,
I will pick raspberries. There, I will make a toast to Kitty with gin,
among flowers like her.

In Memory of Japey Guenther, Who Changed My Life

and to think my first thought of you
was a meditation on the back of your head
from where I sat, ten years old, in the far church pew
awkward, sheltered, too smart for my own good –
I contemplated the presence of the family of strangers
in your row, wondered what the guest singers might do
to impress my bored imagination.
then, you stood to sing, brown shiny hair and all freckles
I was yours forever when you opened your big mouth,
the whole congregation was riveted
by the big voice from such a small guy.
after, I chased you down with a scrap of the evening's program
for an autograph. shyly, I jotted down my address.
If you aren't afraid to write a girl, write to me.
I've got to get to the car, you said.
To avoid being flogged with compliments.

I had to look up *flogged* in the dictionary. at ten,
I spent Saturdays in the library, but I couldn't match
your mind. I spent part of my life trying to catch up to your speed
sharpened my intellectual skills so I could hobnob with you.
we practiced our deceptive skills on long afternoons of
prank phone calls, pretended we were mannequins in the museum.
sometimes we would pick someone at random, and pretend
we thought he was a celebrity. we gave our allowance money out
in arcades, just to watch people diving for quarters.

John, that was you, that child God brought to me, perhaps the
only gift of church I found – the others gifts that could be there,
I had to pry open with a trowel, on my own, flashlight under the blanket,
turning the thin pages of the Bible. we looked for God together,
to see if we could find ourselves in the pages of the Book,
discovered that Christ's favourites were outcasts,
so we must be his favourites, too.

you were my first pillar besides God and Mother. you took from me
the lonely ache of a mixed-up childhood
replaced it with love and laughter.
we looked for ourselves the world over, reading philosophers and
quizzing ministers on the afterlife, we pored through galleries
to see glimpses of ourselves.
you were my first soul mate, and my first fumbling kiss.

➤

once in church you passed me a note that said, thank you
for being my mirror. it's a reflection I was honoured to have, to be held up
to such brilliance,
to be seen.
you were the first one to ever see me. this mirror
gave me strength to find life, to find it on my own terms,
to find it in the ups and downs of manic depression,
to unearth it from the thick soils that buried it.
we could hide from the taunts of meaner children
in the refuge of one another, we could reclaim ourselves
from all the places we'd gone missing.

21 years went by, with you at my side.
and if you couldn't be at my side, your letters filled my in-box
with inspirations and dreams. you never failed to encourage
my creativity, to accept me where others saw a discrepancy.
sometimes you needed my help to sort through hopelessness
and I would share my poems to help you see.

it's unreasonable for me to be angry
when cancer will take one in three.
it is unreasonable to feel alone now that you are gone
when I have everything, my health, the imagination you blessed,
a home and friendships.
it is unreasonable when I know that now
you can be with me every minute, without the boundaries
of geography.

I received the news when I was at my parent's place,
the same sky sprinkling stars over the field where we had once
seen UFOs. How we had hoped that aliens were real,
that we weren't the only ones who didn't fit this planet!
how many hours we spent in these halls, giggling into pillows so
we wouldn't wake my folks.
how the night stretches beyond the furthest farm.
I can only give you to God's hands, now that mine can't reach you.
my first anchor in this world has been cut, and
I am free falling into an endless sky.

Walking the Dark

I can teach you the sound of trains
and how time shatters and restores
and you have taught me
what the heart can hide.

Mixed-river heart –
how do I leave
that which has become
as bread and water?
When the blackbirds fly home,
I may be among them.

I have no obligation to tell you who I am
but I warned you what would become of us
I said, do you remember?
I will be gone before I am gone
How I am crashing how the world is whirling
how my anxious arms are lead
how the abyss, dismal and tacky,
has my future.
I told you I am dizzy and I need help standing up
how I'm tired of tragic tragedies
of drama queens and picket lines
how the sea reclaims its tears
how freedom binds me in promises I can't believe.

these hands have touched the sea at either shore the dust and
the desert and the tar and the snow and the savage smile of
God they have hurt and helped and hitchhiked and they have
touched men and women saints and whores they have opened
doors and shut doors they have made bread and they have
made love but they have never made me happy

I cut myself on scorpions to find your heart
You asked to look inside me
and I turned away.

I couldn't find you for the longest time
our distance was the darkest room
Now you pace the roads as if they were cages
How peculiar our borderlines!
The blanket that held your sleep so softly
knows only the brittle tapestry of bones.

The Disappearing

You collect things
because you are dying of loneliness
imagine my view from here:
watching you fall.

I've watched you with endless fascination.
You are crazy and beautiful and elegant and clever,
complicated, heartbreaking and mad.
I don't think you will ever trust me:
nothing ever belonged to you, so how could I?

Just when I think I can't survive another loss,
I lose you:
you disappear into your shattered emotions,
highways without names, provinces of madness.
The room you left behind is filled with holes, like my heart,
drywall torn open as you hunted for hidden cameras,
the way my husband did before he died.
You unearthed nothing, pawing through the ceiling fixtures,
desperate to figure it out, uncover the plot, sort out the experiment you have
become.
Convinced that forks were microphones, you wrapped them in towels and buried
them, surreal shrouds I found after you disappeared.

People have to leave their sons and lovers and mothers if those
people won't leave meth. My life was a nightmare of spies and hospitals
for too long, I watched my husband sink and die:
and you loved meth more than you loved him, your best friend,
more than anything, more than life, more than me.
Not because I wanted to, you told me as I dropped you off at detox. You
were sobbing. This kind of death is hell. No one wants that. It's an accident, a
poisoning, a nightmare no one can fix. You fled from there – convinced they
would kill you. I cried and cried
whole rivers have run dry
I cry for my husband, the sanest person in the universe,
whose mind was tricked by crystal,
who taped the keyholes shut to keep the watchers out,
eventually didn't know who I was,
but knew they were coming for him.
I wasn't going to find you, too, dead on the floor:
you promised me
companionship, comfort, memories. I believed you could be free:
the man who went before you said, brother, listen to me.

➤

The Astronaut's Wife

Now you are missing, and I tell the police tearfully, please,
please check the ditches and dumpsters and empty barns.
I fear your fear finally found you, the plot thickened until you blew your brains
out to stop the voices from their laughter, their plans, the demons finally gave
you the gun.
I pray they'll find you, alive, so we can have another chance to survive this hell.
I think of your wild-eyed fear the last time I saw you, so sure
you would find something in the wall you clawed apart, a sign that
would tell you what it was all for.

I'll tell you what it was for:
Nothing, my friend, this was all for nothing,
the termites and bugs you saw on your skin and the marks they made
red angry welts, 'speed bumps'.

Take another little piece of my heart, now, baby.
Nothing but garbage,
which is probably where you are,
sometimes a scar is just a scar.

Last August

You shut out the day
with the back of your hand
shielding your eyes from the rest of your life.
For the rest of mine, I will remember the sinister sound
of that knock on my door.

It's 3 a.m. and I know before I open it
that you are dead,
that the day I have feared for so long has come.
The boy who has found you is pale and scarred – he doesn't know
what to do from here, and nor do I:
I stand still and feel the weight of the darkness
carving its black claws into my heart.

They try to revive you with machines and drugs:
the cops mill around surveying the scene.
It's no use, I tell them and my voice is small.
I braced myself a million times
but kept hoping anyways.
I recall how in this very spot that you lay how vividly you
spilled your dreams of Argentina – how no one believed you could do it.
But I knew you could, I believed in you, I told you so,
I knew you could make it, slippery and unnoticed over borders
without passport, I said you had it in you to be a bigger revolutionary
than your idols Manu Chau or Che.
I said, *you can get there if you give up the drugs.*

Now I watch them zip you up and take you down the stairs.
I can't wrap my head around your absence.
I don't know how you could do this to me,
and I don't know how this damn world can possibly survive without you.

The Crystal Ball

What is most true here, at the end of the world
is that I cannot endure your absence.
Your essence is carved out of the earth,
endless, as vast as an empty sky.

I imagined it a million times,
how solemn cops would press my upper arm
with gentle authority. There were always sirens
there where we made our home,
where the familiar turning of the streetcar found Gerrard.
This summer, those sirens sang for you.

I'm terrified of losing the memory of your voice
the way I can't conjure up your scent.
I didn't wash your sweaters for months,
but now every trace is gone regardless.
I'm not counting the promises you made to me and broke
because you gave me more than anyone can or will,
but I can't forgive you for choosing death instead of me,
you who loved life.

I wanted you to take my brother out to sea
and show him all the world. He listened so carefully
to all your stories of Central America, of Africa and Germany.
He thought you would show him how to find sacred plants in South America
on a boat you built yourself. Now all you can show him
are a thousand pictures of your pipe,
how obsessively you photographed that thing, and
filled boxes with shot after shot, the pipe from this angle, and from that.
You thought there were codes in the smoke, that crystal was a crystal ball –
and I said yes, here how the smoke curls I can see those witches dancing
and the demons,
I warned you that this was a sign of what was happening to you,
of madness,
that you were looking into hell because you were going to die.

It doesn't take a hit of crystal meth
to see your future,
written as clearly as it came to pass.

The Astronaut

I know that you feared nothing, not even death,
you were not even afraid as it was coming, creeping stealthily from behind,
there was no fear on your face, just a half-smile,
you didn't even see it come through the door

well, that's just fine if you wanted to die
but I know you only wanted to live, loving life and never fearing it
the way the rest of us did, you were the one who did everything,
tried everything, loved everything.
you would have preferred another thousand adventures,
you wanted to see every country and frontier of land and air, and
you braved inner space with any tool, plant or pill you could find.
you believed that we are astronauts who should explore the borders of the soul
by any means necessary, without terror.
you were a shaman of sorts, sailing across the world to find
the heart of all the people in it, and then finally, to find and claim mine.
you were, with me, one to rage
against dying light.

You should have died on the sea: with the salt air as incense
and the waves as the choir.
how dare you leave your shell for me to find
on the kitchen floor.

because, you bastard, some of us are afraid of the things that you were not
we can't just go on without you,
we tried to keep your soul here, hold you back from the inevitable demise
but we could not fight for you, a soldier who never thought he would go down,
the astronaut who thought he'd never find the edge.

Jesus wept,
and poets lost their poetry that day,
rory was doing the Tibetan last rites in the front room
and the sun blazed hot enough to set the earth on fire
sailors drowned on every sea
and the rain began and rained a thousand days

and since that day I haven't stopped crying
and since that day I haven't stopped dying
how dare you go so gentle into that good night.

THE END

Many of these poems have appeared in magazines and small-press literary publications. Every effort has been made to mention all publications. My apologies to anyone I missed.

Yemaya appeared in Issue 33 of *Hecate's Loom and Wyrd*, Spring 1996.
She appeared in *Siren*, Summer 1996 and *Aphrodite Gone Berserk*, 1996.
Eulogy for Carmine Lowe appeared in *Quarry Magazine*, Volume 45 #3
and *American Poets and Poetry*, March 1998.
Daily Bread appeared in *Ink Magazine*, 1995 and *Tight*, 1996.
Next Door appeared in *White Wall Review*, 1997.
The Bus Poem appeared in *Rattle*, Volume 3 #1 and in Volume 4 Issue 2 of *Zygote*.
It is Only Now appeared in *Prairie Winds*, Spring 1999.
Bad appeared in *Phoebe: an Interdisciplinary Journal of Feminist Scholarship*,
SUNY, 1996.
Elegy appeared in *Sidewalks*, Spring 1999 and in *Other Voices*, Spring 1998.
Portrait of Elaine in the Sun appeared in an unknown issue of *The Outreach*.
Star appeared in Volume 27 of *Oh! Magazine*.
Poem for A. appeared in Winter 1999 of *Main Street Rag*.
New Orleans Jazz Bar appeared in *Diviners*, Fall 1998.
Incest appeared in *Caffeine*, Issue 4.
Distraction and *Memory from Louisiana* appeared in Fall 1996 of *Canned Phlegm*.
Flowers from Carmine appeared in *Damaged Goods*, Issue 1.
Fifteen appeared in *Poet's Page*, April 1998.
Damage and *Everything Tastes Like Crack* appeared in
The People's Poet Anthology 2.
In Memory of Japey Guether, Who Changed My Life; Grief, and
Another Poem for Julie Ann appeared in the anthology
listening to the birth of crystals, edited by Alan Corkish and Andrew Taylor.

About the Poet

Lorette C. Luzajic began her literary explorations shortly after her sister Steph taught her to read *Andy the Church Mouse Learns About Prayer*. She played hooky from kindergarten to type up little stories on her Fisher-Price typewriter. At age 12, her story *Meet Me at the River* won a prize in a young writer's contest. Fittingly, the story was about death.

Lorette continued writing and tried to fit as many other things into the years as possible. She drifted across North America for a few years in a truck named The Camel. She started the world of work pumping gas, worked as a phone psychic and coffee barista, spent nearly ten years in most facets of the book industry, graduated from Ryerson University School of Journalism, edited the online arts mag *The Idea Museum*, and now freelances her writing services and creative products.

Reading remains a primary passion, allowing theoretical foundations for her dabbling in yoga, nutrition, cooking, Simpsons, psychology, world and ancient religions, and art. Now Lorette spends most of her time writing or creating mixed-media artworks that she shows and sells online and at local exhibits. Today she lives in Toronto with her three cats Moses, Uncle Murky, and Knerpie.